TISHYA KUMAR is a student who's extremely passionate about helping others and fighting for rights. She currently lives in Malaysia, which is a common area for refugees to flee to. Tishya's school offered refugees a fantastic teaching programme, allowing her to gain experience and work with them directly.

Tishya also takes part in Model United Nations, which helped to spark her interest in helping others who are not fortunate enough to help themselves.

I am A
Refugee

Tishya Kumar

SilverWood

Published in 2019 by SilverWood Books

SilverWood Books Ltd
14 Small Street, Bristol, BS1 1DE, United Kingdom
www.silverwoodbooks.co.uk

ISBN 978-1-78132-866-8

British Library Cataloguing in Publication Data
A CIP catalogue record for this book is available from the British Library

Page design and typesetting by SilverWood Books
Printed on responsibly sourced paper

This book is dedicated to all the refugee children and their families, especially the wonderful children I met while creating this book. I'd like to thank my school and family for being so supportive!

Being a refugee means that I was forced to leave my country as it is unsafe for me to be living there.

I once lived in my own country and never thought that I would be forced to move.

I remember my parents telling me that it was too dangerous for me to go to school and that soon we would have to flee* the country.

I never thought such a thing would happen to me.

* flee – run away from a place or situation of danger.

In the process of getting here, my parents had to send me by myself, because we didn't have enough money to send the whole family. I haven't seen them in 5 years.

I had to take a risky boat ride all alone. I was denied sanctuary* in many different countries.

* denied sanctuary – to not be allowed safe stay in a country.

I am now living safely in a refugee centre, but I miss my family every single day. I hope that one day I can see them again.

Now I am learning English, Maths and Science in the centre. I really want to be a doctor when I grow up, and go back home and treat my family and friends there.

It just didn't make sense to me. The war was not my fault. Why was I being treated like it was? Bringing me into your country will not cause a war in your country. I'm just a child...

After all, I'm no less human than anyone else in the world.

A MESSAGE TO PARENTS

I wrote this book because I believe that the education of refugees is extremely important, as they can be productive members of society, if they are given the same provision of education as we are. They should be treated as migrants, and there should be a production of safer transportation for those from war-torn countries in order to safely make it to a country in which they would be protected.

Along with child protection, I feel that it is extremely important to also have measures to protect family members of these children, as giving these children a childhood as normal as possible will lead to an outcome of children who can benefit the community that they join.

I decided to write this as a children's book because of how important it is to educate children on refugee rights! Children are the future generation and need to be educated on such dire problems. It's up to us to change the situation and I hope that my contribution will raise awareness and help as many refugee children as possible.

Thank you for reading this book and helping me in my journey to change the lives of children in need.

Tishya Kumar
Author

www.ingramcontent.com/pod-product-compliance
Lightning Source LLC
Chambersburg PA
CBHW041635040426
42447CB00021B/3499

9 781781 328668